Black Irish

Poems

Michele Madigan Somerville

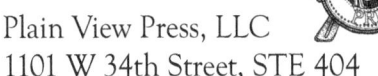

Plain View Press, LLC
1101 W 34th Street, STE 404

www.plainviewpress.net
Austin, TX 78705

Copyright Michele Madigan Somerville 2010. All rights reserved under International and Pan-American Copyright Conventions. No part of this book may be reproduced or distributed in any form or by any means, or stored in a data base or retrieval system, without written permission from the author. All rights, including electronic, are reserved by the author and publisher.

ISBN: 978-0-9819731-3-5
Library of Congress Control Number: 2009937244

Cover art reproduces a painting by Maureen Mullen,
    The Tenacity of Buds
Cover design by Susan Bright
Author's photo: Greg Fuchs

Acknowledgements

The author thanks the following people for their contributions to support of this work: J. Max Robins; Jack, Maria and Grace Robins-Somerville; Gregg Somerville; Sean Somerville, Charles Aaron, Tristin Aaron, Susan Bright, Peter Catapano, Louise Crawford, Jill Eisenstadt, Bill Evans, Merry Fortune, Polly Frost, Greg Fuchs, Ian Ganassi, Jody Gilman, Larry Honig, Kim Hughes, Michael S. Kirkpatrick, Pam Knight, Adam Klein, Sharon Mesmer, Maureen Mullen, Nava Renek, Thaddeus Rutkowski, Joanna Sit, Christopher Stackhouse, Bob Stein, Mike Sweeney, Patricia Sweeney, Tony Towle, "Ruddy girls" and "Ruddy lads," and her many friends at St. Augustine Church in Brooklyn.

"Portrait of A Woman with Her Marker" received First Place prize in the year 2000 W. B. Yeats Society Poetry Competition (NYC) and appeared in *Hanging Loose* 78. "Bodies of Water" appeared in the on-line journal, *Pagan Place* in 2001. Sections in the poem "Four Green Fields" are borrowed, in good faith, from the lyrics of "Four Green Fields" by Tommy Makem.

for
Mary Madigan (1900 -1995)
Bernadette Somerville (1936 - 2008)
Scott T. Somerville (1959 - 2004)

*Cast your mind on other days
That we in coming days may be
Still the indomitable Irishry.*

from "Under Ben Bulben"
W.B. Yeats

Contents

Sorry, Mary	9
Mary Christmas	16
Portrait of a Woman with Her Marker	18
Four Green Fields	20
Kid Madigan	33
Pressure and Heat	34
Love Poem	37
Vale of Cashmere	42
Atonement: I Swing This Bird in the Shape of a Halo . . .	43
Lately, I Have Been Trying To Be More	46
Quinceanera	47
Slow Air	55
Bodies of Water	67
Boob	72
Le Ballon	80
Confessor (You Too)	83
Fighting Irish	89
Capularis	103
The Other Side	112
About the Author	115

Sorry, Mary

Sorry, Mary, you never got the funeral you'd have wanted.
Sorry, Mary, you never got the funeral you deserved.
There should have been bagpipes, step dancers, jigs and reels.
There should have been a fine over-long procession, and a parade
of sad speeches, one more grand than the next
There should have been stoic salutes in bleary abundance.
A big handsome priest named Francis
Xavier with half-a-load on, full of pomp and
bluster should have presided.
He should have marched 'round all sides
of your lavish box, Mary, swinging
his pendulous aromatic thurible as one might a purse.
Sorry, Mary, you didn't get the Mass of Christian Burial
you deserved, and about the rental priest, Mary,
who began the homily: "I didn't know Mary but …"

Sorry the man you loved most with
a passion had to fight for the chance
to march up to the altar of the spare, cheap,
Protestant-looking sanctuary, in order to offer up
a few fond words, Mary, in your honor.
And you should know, Mary, Himself had to cross
both his mother and the priest to do it!
The bishops still don't go in for laughter and poetry
over the stiff. ("Save it for the pub" is their thinking.)
And you know how hard that is, Mary,
for an Irishman to cross both his mother *and* a priest.
You would have liked Himself up there in a new white shirt,
making his mother fidget and the old priest squirm,
prompting everyone else in the sanctuary to laugh, and weep,
on account of that blarney of his, Mary.

Sorry you didn't get the send-off you would have wanted, Mary.
Sorry you didn't get the funeral you deserved.
At least you got to wear that royal blue number one last time,
the one you wore the day Himself was married.

You looked so smart in it, and it was perfect for the occasion.
The wedding was grand, but the marriage
didn't stick, Mary; that's hard
when the groom's queer. I'm afraid
the cosmetician didn't do a very good job on you Mary,
for discreet in all else, you never were when it came
to face paint. 'Twas black brows and fire
engine red to set off your ice
blue eyes. You would have flown
into a bloody rage over the lipstick! Scarlet not
salmon was for your mouth, Mary.
Though the water-color decades of those Spanish
crystals winding *Ave Marias* and
Pater Nosters round your locked
fingers were familiar in a lovely way,
the hands seemed someone else's.
I will say this much for you, Mary —
you finally got a proper manicure.
The girl didn't have to yell at you,
that last time, to wait for the final coat
to dry. You looked alright there in the box, Mary,
vain, elfin New Yorker, though
it's hard to look
your best, Mary,
when the soul has taken leave
of your senses.

Sorry Mary, you got carried away
by six guys that came with the package.
Pall bearers for hire is how it's done these days.

Sorry Mary, that your buckos Matt and Max and Scott
never got to haul your box down the aisle.
But you would have liked the casket, Mary,
lovely and too ornate; upon it were all twelve
apostles, seated at a grand table in a row,
getting drunk, or so it's easy to imagine,
the bunch of them out tying one on
with Our Lord on a Thursday night!

And forgive us, Mary, for burying you
from an unattractive church.
Saint John's was where you dutifully dropped
your weekly fiver in the shake-down basket,
where the priest was a thief but not wholly
without charm. At least his elegant tastes
extended to keeping the little Yorkville sanctuary
well-maintained and full of fresh-
cut fragrance, a place where God
wouldn't mind stopping and sitting
a spell on a hot day in the luminous climate-
controlled dark. 'Tis indeed a shame we buried you
from a church you never entered vertically, Mary.

Truth is, Mary, Saint Pat's would have been the proper spot.
And the Cardinal himself should have been on hand
to shake that morning star over your box,
holy water springing forth from its head,
for if you didn't deserve a resounding "Yea,
though I walk through the valley of
the shadow of death" psalm and dance
amid the tenebrous resplendence
of the cathedral, I'll be damned
if I know who might!
I'm sorry for the bland absence of song.

I'm sorry Mary, that more verse wasn't declaimed
into the November chill, as, leaning upon spades,
the Gate of Heaven diggers maintained a respectful
distance and your clan tossed carnations in a heap
which spilled onto the astro-turf blanket. Sorry, Mary,
your poet maintained a respectful
distance, for there ought to have been
encomium and threnody galore!
There should have been elegiac couplets by the score!
And dirges, and laments and monody and what's more —
the poet you so well loved should have roared
like a banshee of old: Cast a cold eye on life,
on death — but before ye pass by, have another,
Horseman, just a wee drop, to keep you
warm for the long trip home. *Slainte*, Horseman.

Sorry, Mary, you didn't get the funeral you'd have wanted.
Sorry, Mary you didn't get the send-off you deserved.
O Mary, your funeral should have been great *craick*!
There should have had bagpipes and reels,
there should have been an Irish tenor, Mary,
to sing *Ave Maria My Wild Irish Rose*!

Sorry we couldn't all go down to Finegan's
on the corner of First Avenue, Mary.
I'm sorry that skinflint greenhorn who owned the joint,
the one who saw you come in each Saturday night
for three decades running, Mary,
never once bought you a drink on the house,
not even on your 85th birthday.

That cheap donkey bastard should have
bought you a drink, Mary,
because you spent a lot of money in that place,

and always left at 20% or more for the girl.
And I'm sorry no one got drunk at your wake, Mary,
not even those of us who are still allowed.
If you'd died a decade earlier,
when your number was still RE-4-8010,
before your daughters had declared war
with one another, a war between the states
of stubbornness and pettiness,
everyone would have been in his cups.
But that was before so many saw the light
And converted, from Catholicism
to A.A. Sorry, Mary, no one got drunk at your wake.
You wouldn't have approved of that,
but men, these days, are better now,
they like to clean up and fly straight,
take care of their children,
stick around awhile —

Sorry, Mary, you never got the funeral you deserved.
But I'm not sorry you stuck around 'till '95.
I'm glad I had the chance to straighten you out on
your fear, that a good man might be barred
from Heaven. What I mean to say is sometimes,
if the world had beaten a man down — sometimes,
if a man wasn't in his right mind —
In other words, newsflash, Mary;
they were now letting the suicides into Heaven, Mary.
You protested when I told you so:
  "No. Go on!" — your voice inflected with both
doubt and the unmistakable rising
pitch of optimistic incredulity ascending
with bright lyric force, inclining towards faith —

"Don't believe me, Mary? Ask the rummy priest who rounds.
The Cardinals changed the rules! A man who died
in a moment of weakness, by his own hand, if
he was truly sorry, Mary, could
now enter the Gate of Heaven."
("Are you *sure?*")

I'm glad you lived long enough, to believe, Mary,
that your man might indeed tip his cap while bidding
Peter,"Top'a'th'mornin' to ye!"
before passing through those Gates
like a poor man through the eye—
Aye, I'm a little bit sorry
you didn't make it to 100.
That would have been something, Mary,
and knowing you'd beaten your sister Bridget
to the century finish might have made the victory double sweet.
You were tired. But I am glad
you stuck around long enough to learn that
sometimes, Mary, even God has a change of heart.

Sorry you didn't get the funeral you deserved, Mary,
but I'm not sorry you stuck around 'till '95.
It was a terrific honor, to watch you fail
to crack, Mary, after you were spirited
away from East 73rd and then stashed up in Franny's.
What great *craick* it was to smuggle a wee dram
past the crocked security guard,
to perch in your nursing home rocker,
to pull a laugh out of you
by dubbing your portable commode
"the cocktail table," as we sipped and gabbed
about news and weather without the TV on.

I'm sorry you didn't get the funeral you deserved, Mary.
I'm sorry your life was so full
of shadow and death, but I'm not sorry
you stuck around as long as you did, Mary,
for it was an honor to sit with you as you died.
How lucky was I to have you just long enough,
to behold that wild dimming sprite in you,
the hard-boiled fairy,
so steadfast and so alive
as it leapt,
out of you
and dove
down
into the tiny
gut of my girl,
who is called "Maria," Mary.
How sorry can I possibly be?
How can I be sorry you stuck —
How can I be sorry you stuck around
so long Mary, when I can glance across
my kitchen table, on any given night,
and watch my girl as she gnaws the wing
of a chicken, or catch her as she knits
a feral Black Irish brow,
and gasp, as I bear
witness, in disbelief, or belief —
it hardly matters which —
and laugh as I exclaim in
whispered astonishment,
"My God, my God,
will you look at her?
It's Mary!"

Mary Christmas

Unconstrained by Yuletide spirit, she
complained each year of the hundred
Christmas cards from those expecting
replies. Too old at 90, she was, at last,
at last, too old to shop, to burrow,
blue head tucked through the mob
through the crowd waiting for the bus
up 2nd or down 3rd, too old for wrenching
sale items from grips of Alexander's
denizens yet not too old to hobble
over to First National for fresh-smelling Christmas
Club tender, crisp currency to slide into
cards with holes for presidents to peek through,
and she was and just
the right age for taking care of Father Peyton
who "writes to me personally," (dixit Mary
who then lacked knowledge of photocopying
mechanisms and all computers made and would make
possible. Mary was young and spry enough to remember
to stake Saint John's, Saint Jean's, the Maryknolls,
the Blue Army Rosarians, Holy Name Society,
Knights of Columbus and a host of other sanctioned
solicitors far too numerous to name who, come Advent,
step up their shake-down efforts and target the venerable
in honor of Baby Jesus and his teen mom.
O, what radiance I beheld in Mary
those nights of her last decade
when I would bear the so-called "tree" up
her four flights immediately following the Feast of
the Immaculate Conception, and present myself
at her door bearing a tiny Saturnalia bush.
Generally I found Mary nursing "a vodka" with
"Live at Five" on loud. She'd trot into the kitchen, fill
a rocks glass with screw-top Chablis and push the low-
ball glass it into my hand, scowling, as I set
the squat botanical reject down atop the television set.
"Now why d'ye go wastin' yer money on that?"

Shaking her head, she'd think, 'Who
but a spendthrift drops 20 dollars on an agricultural gift?
A gift soon to be dead, a present
stupid as flowers?' Saying "Take that bloody thing
home with you" always made her feel better
about my seasonal blunder for a spell,
but she'd return to this consternation
throughout the visit, from her perch in the rocker,
elaboration on the condemnation:
"I don't need it." You could always tell
how much Mary liked a gift by how stubborn
she was in her effort to give it back.
Each year, it was always the same.
Mary rocked, quaffed and chastised
as I hooked tinted balls upon gummy limbs
and striped mint upon prickly branches
and cheap angels among half-
desiccated needles and strung garlands and pearly
green beads and affixed gold wires that held together
red velvet bows upon the lame-ass boughs
of the bush which, once adorned, became a near
tree sufficiently towering, in theory if not in practice,
to over-power her elfin Bridget Ebenezer self
causing Mary to change her tune! "Oh!"
Herself would cry out, "Will ye look at it?
It's Bah-Yoo-ti-ful!" Tilting her glass, bending into
a toast to the oncoming season and year, Mary
would call out "Slainte!" and "Merry Christmas!"
(way too early in Advent). Protracting her
syllables more and more as the bit of wine
over-loosened her mouth, she stretched
out her words. A glassy luster overtook her
pleasure-squinted eyes, and lasted most of the visit.
But she could not hold on to it. Herself could not allow
the evening to end without getting a bit more scolding in:
"I can't carry that bloody thing to the garbage," she'd carp.
"You'll have to come back to take it out by the first
of the year or the Feast of the Epiphany."

Portrait of a Woman with Her Marker

Thinking it a fine joke in the autumnal chill,
having gotten a pair of vodka martinis into the old
girl, Mary, 85 in 1985, which left her flushed and
flustered, wild-eyed and elfin amid the greenery,
he posed her where angels fear, saying
"Come on, Mary, how about a quick one
with your arm thrown 'round the stone?"
She'd thought of having the rock
inscribed well in advance of taking occupancy
below, of having the name carved in beforehand,
but the daughters said it was "tacky."
"That'll just have to wait until you're gone."
(Would you jump into my grave that fast?)
Mary was afraid someone might take her dark
spot in the common ground among the faithful
departed, among the consecrated bones of erstwhile
communicants; among the Evanses, McKennas, O'Briens,
and Rooneys, among the Heaveys, O'Haras, Kennedys and Killarneys,
in the company of Mulligans, Fitzgeralds and Molloys,
O'Learys, Donohues, Riordans and Kinanes.
among Kinsellas and Costellos, for all her days
among DiGiornos, Dippolitos, Lucacentis,
Mandoranos and Falcones, and Capuccis, Ruggieros,
Trovatos and Mazzones. She was afraid of
someone looking to cut the line at the Gate
of Heaven cemetery, of someone coveting her
place within the verdant realm, someone
waiting to descend into her dug out
hollow in Valhalla's hallowed ground
which contains remains of her
mate, gone at 50, by his own hand;
daughter dead of childbirth at 22,
son, drove off a bridge at 30,
girl, dead at 2, buried for Christmas —

Black Irish Mary with her way
(of all flesh), her cold eye cast "Come on,
smile Mary, darlin'! How about a quick shot
of you and the headstone
for good measure?"

Four Green Fields

for Gregg

In the middle of the summer,
in the middle of the month,
in the middle of the last year of the life
of the first Catholic president —
squared-jawed second son
of an Irishman — a second son
was born to my father.
"What'd'ya do?" called Dick
from down the opposite end of the Caryl Inn?
"Name the kid 'Gregory' after the Pope?"
"Name's not 'Gregory.'
Just 'Gregg'."

On the night
of the child's birth,
as the mingling of spirit and
meat and light was taking place
and the world was drawing a fresh soul
into its irrevocable spasmodic din,
pulling the boy forward,
he sensed the soft brute
propulsion of his own
ferocious soul hungry for light
putting the squeeze on him,
and the rhythmic work of his
mother against his flesh:
its loosening and tightening
upon him; he made his way
toward the true light which leads
to death by the muscular dint
of ordinary miracle;
the sire of the second son, sprang
for a round for the bar.

Fractured illumination leapt;
glints flickered like votives in rows
of curved whiskey glass;
a veil of smoke lay softly over
the amber gin mill pall of the Caryl Inn
where the father of Gregg had killed
the pain of labor and delivery.

Dick, down the bar, sent roses
to the hospital, but not the father
of the newborn second son.
Even if money was tight,
a guy "on the job" could always
pick up a dozen roses "on the arm"
on the occasion of the birth of a son —
the labor was short, the delivery
"unremarkable." A fine son
was bouquet enough
for the sturdy girl
who had no need of roses.
Irish girls were made for birth:
one a year, God willing,
according to "Father."

She'd given the father two sons now,
sons enough to make up for that
poor showing first time out.
A firstborn girl is no man's desire.
A man needs sons. A girl is cute,
so long as plenty of sons follow.
But men make sons,
and the second son would be all
the first was not!
There'd be nothing slow
about this one. The second would be quick
to football and words, fast

on his feet, and smart
as the girl, God damn 'er.
Best of all, he would not grow up
to be a sissy or a broad.

I had four green fields, each of them a jewel
But strangers came and tried to take them from me
I have fine strong sons, who fought to save my jewels
They fought and died, and that was my grief, said she.

When the time came for
the child to be called in Baptism,
the priest raised an objection.
"The child must bear
the name of a saint."
The diminutive "Gregg"
was not enough.
So the middle son was called
to Christ by the name "Michael."
"Michael" after the angel clad
in armor and boots;
"Michael," archangel, Chief
of Seraphim, pug of the firmament,
Heaven's bouncer, God's rough
draft, God's second shot,
"Michael," patron saint of cops.

"Who gives this child in Baptism?"
The square-jawed brother-in-law
who had cheated on his toddler
as her mother lay dying of
giving birth stood up to speak.
"I do."

Said the mistress
of the brother-in-law
to the wife as she lay dying:
"You will
be dead, soon, and
I will be living
with your husband,
raising up your girl."

He was a creep, but
he was a Catholic
creep and therefore adequate
to serve as holy proxy
to whom it would fall
to usher the newborn child
toward the fire of the dove.

Only half-Irish, the father of Gregg Michael
hated the Irish: Irish men were pussies
who let their wives chase them
'round the kitchen with the frying pan
and made them slap
the paycheck down on the table every Friday!
The newborn was Irish but he wasn't
going to grow up to be
some beaten-down Paddy
who'd let some Donkey bitch get him
by the shorthairs.

Children was woman's work, and the second-
choice of godfather to the second
son was a "stand-up guy."
"He had a pair of balls on him."

No sooner was that bride safe in the sod
than that dapper widower was dropping
the child with his sturdy sister
(An Irish girl always knows what to do
with an extra child.) and running
off to Florida with the swine
who deserved him.

The godfather of Gregg Michael
would get a fresh start,
a clean slate.
Widowhood left him
free as a vulture.
The square-jawed dandy
with his well-pressed suit,
and a couple of bucks in his pocket
had a long life ahead of him,
and he was free to spend it
half in the bag.

For Jesus is as lenient
as the Church fails to be.
The saint's name "Michael"
was a tribute to both
the second son's
grandfather and the blood
uncle: who was first
choice for a godfather,
a sailor who could not
make his way across the sea
in time to appear
before the font
so as to speak
what sacred promises
the infant could not.

On the day of the Christening,
it's likely I shifted, half-numb
feet in stiff plastic Mary-
Janes, patent-leather party
shoes — itching in a church frock
of pink, a crinoline scratching
underneath. I had grown
tired of commotion surrounding
the baby the baby the baby the baby
the baby this the baby that.
"Be quiet" was an injury and a bore.
I craned to glimpse him, so
ridiculous in a dress —
I'm surprised the old man went for that:
a boy in a dress.
"Who will answer for this child?"
"I will."
"Michael, do you renounce Satan
and the glamour of Evil?"
"I do renounce him,"
the brother-in-law answered,
"And all his empty promises?"

Not even the surge of the Holy Sprit
caused the boy to stir as the man in a dress
anointed the chest of the boy in a dress
laying grease down in the shape of the cross.
Calling him "Michael," "Father"
raised the boy above above the creamy
marble of the holy pool and
the man began in the dress began
to pour water rhythmically, thrice,
over the hairless pate
of the boy in the dress.

Gregg almost slept through his own epiphany,
but as the chill trickled down the round
of his still-soft head, the shock of
the stream awakened him.
The magical boy unloosed
a watery protest, a bubbling wail,
the full-force work of unfinished
lungs. His cries trembled
the shadowy still as they
accompanied the bounding
intonation of the *Ora Pro Nobis,* litany of
the saints, as it ascended from the guts
of the projecting cleric and sifted
serpentine, diffusing upwards
and outwards into
the apse, transepts and nave, winding
its gorgeous twine 'round
pillars of granite, marrying fog
with declining light
of late afternoon as glories pierced
downward through opalescent
glass divvying up
pure light into streaming sectors
which, limited by lead, dispensed emerald,
caramel, sapphire and burgundy
in lavish slants through the rose
window in the Gothic dark
like swords sculpted of dust,
slender, direct, cutting
open the souls of all who were open
to such lightlessness punctuated
by tiny gold tongues of echoing blue-bellied
flame in brass tips atop tall candles:
illumination minuscule,
interruptive in the noctilucent
and consecrated dark, radiant

like God's night sky divided from day,
resounding roundly —

Swinging his thurible, Father unleashed a burning
frankincense and hyssop which sur-
mounted the shadows and penetrated
the dark, flooding the great apse
with fragrance and cloud
which lingered beyond visibility,
and thus the sin the second son was said
to have been born with was washed
away, along with the menace of Limbo;
as if upon grease, unction left
like unction upon on the heart left
in the shape of an X — or cross
upon a wailing throat —

I do remember the contagion
of fidgeting, the clearing
of throats, the tangible tension
of 30 hung-over people
waiting for a drink. It was a Sunday
summer afternoon. Flowers lay
before the *rerodos* before the tabernacle
of gold and shrine to the Virgin,
gladiola, upright as swords and lilies of
white — I want to say Asiatic Stargazers,
too, to tell you their brazen pink
demeanor and sexual nose were
represented for the glory of
God, and raving Tiger
Lilies, too, fierce as Jesus
in his tantrum, turning tables
over in the temple, the beauty of
their God-sculpted biology
all proudly out —

but I can not
in honesty speak
of their loud
dazzling on the day
Gregg was called in Baptism
in the summer of '61
at St. Elizabeth's Church in Washington
Heights, a neighborhood named after a slave-
owning general we call "the father
of our country" by the Irish and
named for the mother of miracle
baby, John the Baptist who was mis-
taken in his time
for the Messiah.

After the church part, it was friends
back to the house, up five flights
on West 190th . There, gals in chokers
of pearl and festive frocks and nylons
with garter hooks and snaps, revealed
when they placed
their maraschino Whiskey
Sours down, as they stooped to lift
diaper-fattened toddlers up from
their spots on the oilcloth floor,
their several scents fusing: Jean Naté,
Four Roses, Vitalis, Aqua Velva, and Cashmere
Bouquet ascending from coifs and wrists
to collide in a stifling clash with living
room Pall Mall clouds and beer, Schaeffer
("when you're having more than one").
A bright ham stuck with cloves sat
front and center, surrounded —
on a folding table by short stacks of Wonder
Bread, potato salad, and cold cuts
arrayed. If anything rotated

on the phonograph it was the Clancy Brothers
singing *The Minstrel Boy* or *Four Green Fields* —

Long time ago, said the fine old woman
Long time ago, this proud old woman did say
There was war and death, plundering and pillage
My children starved, by mountain valley and sea
And their wailing cries, they shook the very heavens
My four green fields, ran red with their blood, said she.

The father of Gregg Michael
didn't write often but he drank like a writer,
kept his typewriter prominently displayed.
He fancied himself "a writer."
He had committed
a few dozen verses by Robert
Service to memory.
He had managed
to type up a chronicle of the times,
a dirty little book with "Revolution"
in its title. The mother of the man's young,
adding her secretarial acumen to the mix,
prepared and submitted
the manuscript to every publisher in New York.
There were nibbles, but
mostly there was rejection.
The would-be author soon gave up
writing, blaming his failure on Jew publishers,
the Donkey wife, "the job," and the Pope
(four brats in five years).
He gave up trying
to hit "the big time,"
he gave up seeking
"fame and fortune."

He gave up working
as a writer, but
he never gave up
drinking like one.
He never gave up
talking about being one,
someday, nor calling himself "a writer."
Sometimes when he was really in the bag
he even called himself "a poet."
"I wish my *sons*," he used to say,
"I wish my sons could string a sentence together
the way you can. I wish my *sons*
had your balls," he used to say
to his first-born, the daughter
named for the Irish grandfather;
called after the gilded angel
clad in armor and boots.
"I wish my sons had your talent,"
he used to say, pulling me close
beside him on the couch,
as I shrinked away,
his whiskey-breath syllables
running dopily together
like a lost train
of thought
into a bog,
his brute nature
all proudly
out. "I wish
any one of my three sons
could write like you.
I wish I could take that
away from you,
and give it to them.
That kind of talent

is wasted
on a woman."

If he had been any kind of a writer,
the father of Gregg Michael
would have understood
the sin in that.
If he had been any kind of a father
he might have thought it
without spelling it out.
If he had been any kind of a writer
the old man would well have known
it doesn't work that way.
Neither donkey wife,
nor "the sauce," nor any
Pope, nor even "the force"
could have kept him from it —
If the father had been any kind of
a poet — it would have taken him up
the Word, in its wings.

*Michael — Michele — Do you
renounce Satan and all his works?
I do renounce him.
And all his empty promises?*

If the man had been any kind of a father,
his daughter would never have torched
those couple of pages of his novel
that night he came in with his load on and loaded his off-
duty revolver for effect,
so that when he stuck it up
against his own head
or that of the mother

of his fine sons,
the result would be dramatic.

If he'd been any kind of a novelist,
it wouldn't have taken three
years for the bad lieutenant
to discover those incinerated pages —
the firstborn's transgression,
("sins of the father")
my unholy blow.

If he'd been any kind of a writer
he would have known
the Muse *is* a "broad,"
fierce and hard
to figure.
What kind of Muse
would waste her song
on the likes of him?
There was no amplitude,
no plenitude, no filling up
with spirit, no inspiration,
no fervor, no Grace, no love
for, nor any modicum of confidence in
the Word. His Muse
never had his back —
and he never had the balls
to stick it out
like his daughter.

Kid Madigan

"Ya *know* how to move your feet. Ya *know* how to snap
out those punches, Michele!" urged the ex-pug, as I wrapped
my hands in cloth and tape, and he laced me up, and I dug
my fingers into the stinking hide and he tugged
the headgear down which held in it an old boxing scent
I found stunning. Tapping gloves, my partner and I commenced,
with sparring. I slipped a few jabs, ducked a right,
but was somewhat frozen in my pose too slow dispensing might —
until that cross landed on the bridge where my nose
would have been and I thought about all the people I loathe,
all the low-life scumbags I'd really like to pound,
and I stepped to the left, before coming around
with a nice hook to the head. How splendid, the desire to kill
with my hands! And feeling like maybe I could — was a thrill!

Pressure and Heat

Marilyn the Tortoise, was bequeathed to my brothers and me in '69
by our drug-dealing Cuban building superintendent
who, running one step ahead of the local Anti-
Crime Unit, was forced to leave his French
Provincial mustard velveteen sectional
sofa and the largest RCA model television
money could buy. He packed up what he could of his tight
cellar dwelling in haste, leaving family pet, Marilyn, behind.
She lived her truncated reptilian existence in a roasting pan
lined with gravel; she ate lettuce when we thought to feed her,
and had little choice but to shit where she ate.
Thinking her dead, one day, we discarded her.
Little did we know, tortoises fly
in the face of time — almost as if death fails
to tunnel into the tender part of their living meat.
Little did we know our Chelonian — our testudine,
Marilyn, descended directly from the Triassic age.
Little did we know the tortoise we neither
named nor renamed might have lived
a hundred years had we not treated her like garbage,
consigning her to a slow death by negligence.
We felt sorry and stupid and full of guilt and
fear at the pediatrician's office as we read up on
tortoises in Children's *Highlights* and discovered
our Marilyn, who had lived a life unmarred
by the vicissitudes of glamour,
might have been hibernating when we left her
for dead. We toyed with imagining
she had surpassed our expectations
by cheating death, that Marilyn had scratched her way
out of the garbage room on those slow claws of hers,
her life preserved, her scutes unscathed, and had
managed to venture down Broadway
to the northernmost limit of Van Cortland Park

where she might graze free in a world more capacious
than the silvery oblong limits of her roasting pan.

The tortoise comes closer than many to deathlessness,
but immortality eludes even these creatures.
"Athanatos" she was not,
though Marilyn Monroe was
sometimes called a "goddess,"
after whom our tortoise was named;
she lacked the carapace that serves
as armor to offer protection from predators.
And though premature death
penetrated Marilyn,
she persisted, ever-
frozen above the grate,
the white skirt of her frock, a butter-cream flourish,
an Elizabethan collar aloft, a circumnavigating
froth about her full hips for our pleasure.
We loved our dumb bomb-
shell blonde. We loved her nude
pinup shots on the beach
where the wind lifted her fair
mess of tresses and caressed her pink
freckled flesh. We loved her gleam, her slow-motion
Milltown ode to her "best friends." Whether heart-
shaped or pear-shaped, it's all coal
converted to ice under the pressure of heat
that wends its way toward the prismatic
luster of the whiteness that is full
of color, improbable and rare. We loved
the genuine blonde whose platinum
came from a bottle. We loved our Marilyn,
more concubine than queen, who captivated us;
we prized our glistening treasure,
more adoring than adored, adorned,
incandescent and ablaze, yet dying

too soon; fated to become a monument.
Marilyn would be 80 today, old as a tortoise,
with brown roots and her cartilaginous flesh gone
grey, but forever sewn into her Happy
Birthday Mr. President gown,
her pink wiggle deliciously bound
in a luminescent mesh like fresh catch
shimmering on a line, her mouth a ring of blood,
translucent as she was transparent,
whom the camera loved,
who developed in the dark, fatherless; orphan
daughter of a madwoman, child-
less child, shuttling from man to
man in search — We loved our serial adulteress,
our heavy-lidded slob, our beaming, extravagant
latecomer, our woeful comedienne, our glittering junkie,
our starlet spawned in Spring who failed to claw
her way to autumn. We loved her breathless baby
timbre and those real tits God gave her. We loved the moist
tenderness of her generous living flesh, her damaged
divinity. We adored our Mrs. DiMaggio, whose
Yankee Clipper left roses on her grave for years
after she took a Louisville slugger to his heart.
We loved the Commander-in-Chief's 'booty call,'
the playwright's fetish, Albert Einstein's wet dream —
and though she was anything but Spartan, we loved her
as some Helen of Troy for our day, the piece of
ass that launched a thousand ships.

Love Poem

O, you are a beautiful brute; your reach is colossal,
your power, undeniable — you even smell good.
You are all over the place, easy
to find, like a lover who, by convenience,
makes up for what he otherwise lacks;
but your incursions are tyrannical. No
sector of my world
as we know it goes untouched
by your might. I am always
making apologies for you;
you embarrass me among my friends,
(especially around the holidays).
They think I'm a lunatic to put up with your
bigotry and deceit. They say you're a crutch.
that you are hard, and you are, hard and cool
as your marble accoutrements. God knows
when it comes to sex, you're twisted;
on one hand you hate it, on the other,
what rival or counterpart more espouses,
more embodies brazen carnality than you?
What other more meaty, more voluptuous, more full?
O, the body unguent is everything with you!
The way in which your passion informs
everything, I admire that — one of your finest traits —
but your perversions abound, so much so
I'm almost inclined to view your flagellation
practices and mortification contraptions
as the healthier part! And as everyone knows,
you treat your women like shit, with none able
to measure up to your ideal, your ballsy Jewess,
your serene May queen of submission,
who sometimes seems to run the show.
It is no secret you do good works;
we all know you heal the sick and feed the poor.
But at what cost? Liberty

means nothing to you,
unless it's your own. Some call you a "mother"
(Though a mother tends to be careful with her young.)
but I think of you more as bad boyfriend.
Sure, I've left a few times, but I come back.
You bank on that; recidivism like mine is your
blessed windfall. You count on all those chumps
who call out for you on their death beds:
penultimate syllables on shallow breath.
They're smart to hedge their bets,
and you're smart too as you jump in for the save,
offering your measure of hope and Extreme Unction —
offering your music of the spheres, and a splash of bourdon bells'
radiating partials, tierce and quint; your *Ave* Maria and
Angelus Bells, with your *Agnus Dei* and most holy pedal and swell
and litany at the font that never fails to shiver
my spine, and your principals, thrones and seraphs
intoning under the great dome of the empyrean;
with your satin chasubles and pendulant thuribles,
with your gold leaf and three-way veneration,
offering promise for new life. You are not easy
to turn away — even with your shakedowns and indulgences,
even with your muscle in the sovereign heart
of the great city to which all roads lead:
wherein your hideous secrets and punitive impulses fester,
where, protected by your Swiss Guard and irrefragable
commission, among the splendor of your *palazzi* and *cappelle*,
you rule. And with your Buonarroti adorning your
ceilings and halls, and your mouthpiece Alighieri
the Great, who could possibly accuse you
of not bringing something to the table?
But it's almost impossible to forgive you
for failing to do justice to the whole idea
behind the "star of wonder" and perpendicular lumber.
For dispensing with the precepts of your great rabbi
so soon after the Mountain of Skulls and empty sepulcher,

so quick on the heels of lift-off at Mount of Olives which
your poet king ascended barefoot, spiriting
the Ark of the Covenant toward the zenith,
at which point the looting began.
Not long ago, I traveled through a blizzard
to hear one of your own servants speak about
The Torah. Old now, wise, and
pissed as Hell at you and
the president, your prophet
raved, as from the pews
arose a protest disguised as a loaded
question regarding clean needles,
rubbers and the spread
of fatal disease. Your Daniel* paused
to ponder before responding.
I waited, wondering,
praying he might take you on.
His gaze traveled upward to the rose
window drafted in reticules of lead and
vitrified glass, ventured next, blearily
round the nave of the cruciform edifice,
surveying the apse, settling on "the stations,"
he craned his neck to fix his focus
upon the elaborate *reredos* behind him
upon which an ark bejeweled with gems
New York's turn-of-the-century poor
forked over, birthstones and rock plucked
from wedding rings, sits,
wherein The Body rests.
But your Daniel refused to go up against you;
his love was too strong,
but he knew silence
would be a sin: "Just because
you can't do everything,"
equivocated your Jesuit,
"doesn't mean you have to do nothing."

But there is so much else to absolve you of:
the Gregories, with their bonfires to protect the world
from the poet of Mytilene, Plato's 10th muse,
European holocaust neutrality in the Modern Age,
your many Inquisitions and *Auto da Fé*,
your executions of heathen by slow
immolation and the multifarious
torments of the rack.
Your cavalcade of larcenous,
butcher Popes, and bishops who rape;
and your freshest blights, rampant
pedophilia and obstruction of justice
pursuant to it; your misogyny and the
homophobia you train on your own
liturgy queens and choirmasters,
without whom there's no you!
Your Teresa in Calcutta, exhorting
women dying of hunger
to breed. Some call you a mother
but I think of you as a bad boyfriend
I can't give up — When you turn me out,
when I work for you, tossing government
beans into emergency food supply sacks,
or when it's my morning
to uphold the body and speak the words
as I look into the radiating eyes of open-
hearted souls on the cue who hold nothing
back as they bring to the table all
they are, all
the confidence in the world, and nothing but
trust in the power of the feast
you call a foretaste of Heaven,
I am capsized by ardor, and flooded
with the voltage of my own adoration,
and its persistent aftershock that resounds;
it's a fine line between terror and exultation.

With your hold on my Irish,
with your John and his "in the beginning
there was The Word … and
The Word was God"
which makes him irresistible
to me — I can not seem
to say "No
way." No,
you can't take have all of me.
You can't have my kids.
My body is mine.
My mind — I'll hang on
to my female *Pater Noster*;
and the apocryphal ideal of those
"drag king" pontiffs Patricia
the scholar told me about, prelates
truly made in God's image. I'll hang on
to my transgender God.
You may be the
winner but you can't take all
of me; my love,
my vice, my rock
dove, my rock,
my dove.

* Rev. Daniel Berrigan, 2005

Vale of Cashmere

Fueling the fire we walk in the rain,
Obstinate (a pair of Irish Francophiles);
Refraining, we skirt the ravine, restrained,
Bewildered amid the wilderness while
Immersed in fecundity, we traverse,
Double bound, the lavish Vale of Cashmere,
Delectably stuck, wondering what's worse,
Ecstasy curbed or the Hell of being near?
Near, as you lay an arm round my shoulder,
Looking upward in that desperate way you do,
Open, shut, seething with the quiet smolder
Venus stokes, so much so, my lone hope is you,
Exactly now, beneath this cool green canopy,
Right here, amid the emerald mist, might kiss me.

Atonement: I Swing This Bird
in the Shape of a Halo 'Round my Head.

For all the times I discarded oatmeal and cheese,
for all the times I asked St. Anthony to locate my cell phone,
for all the times I yawned as my husband
      spoke in over-precise detail about Drudge or *The Wire*,
      for all the times I allowed my eyes to glaze over
      as girlfriends went on about their cretin *beaux*;
      for all the times I threatened my son
      with cessation of Sponge-
bob privileges, when I should have been roasting a chicken
or when I should have been helping the boy with the
         bludgeoning
7th grade homework illiterate borderline personality
Frau Doctor Professor Fink assigns,
when I could have been teaching him something proper,
      like Latin,
or practicing *Scarborough Fair* or *Cockles and Mussels*
(piano homework);
for all the times I talked to boys about poetry
      as if they were geniuses, at parties, because they were "easy
on the eyes"; for my overall immaturity,
      for all the times I put newspapers in regular trash,
      and left the lights on, or brushed my teeth with the water
         running,
      or failed to supervise nightly flossing, or blew
off *Le Petit Prince* or *Catcher in the Rye*
even as the spawn importuned
"Please read to us Mommy!"
Or employed high fructose corn syrup
and brain-masticating cathode rays to reward —
for all the times I couldn't push away the trauma
to which those I've loved have subjected me;
for all the times I haven't been sacrificial enough,
for all the times I throw myself a "pity party"
      about housework.
      "Get off the cross, Mom; we need

the wood for the fire."
For all the times I might have jumped my spouse
and failed to follow through;
for all the times I grew impatient with Bernadette;
for all the times I declined to purge
    the red folder and peruse knapsack contents,
    to attend P.S. 321 Pot Luck events
    and execrable Entenmanns bake sales;
    for all the times I eschewed necessary nagging
    so as to remain beloved in the moment,
    or ragged on the hedge fund Stockholm Syndrome Princess;
    he's not mean, just trapped;
for all the times I've gossiped;
for all the times I hide from my family in the bathtub,
    or laugh at Howard Stern or Sarah Silverman,
    or wear black bra with a white blouse,
    for all the times I fail to be brave,
    I swing the revolving fowl —
    for all the times I say "wassup" or "girlfriend"
    hood-style in the presence of my girls,
for all the times I've blown off bagging cans at the Food Pantry,
    or watched *Sex in the City* reruns
    when I should have been
    marinating a chicken, I swing this bird
    in the shape a halo
    'round my head.
    For that time I ruined 13-year-old Maria's life
    by dancing with my accomplice,
    AKA her father, at Jane's Bat Mitzvah,
    to the 80's R & B of our courtship years,
    in front of kids she knew,
    for all the times I fulminated on Day 24,
    or sought revenge, or made love
    to a grudge, or luxuriated in my
    disgust for real estate developers and flaks
    and ad execs, and republicans;

>   for the time I ogled firemen
>   on the Communion line at the 911 mass;
>   for all the times I wrote to Fuchs in French
>   (*Vers la bas, Garcon!*);
> for all the times I referred to a woman's
>   "married name" as "the slave name,"
> for all my vanity — How the Susan Sontag
>   streak I suspect under-
>   lies my $H_2 O_2$ hair
>   fills me with terror!
> For all those transgressions, I swing
>   this bird round my graying head,
>   in the shape of a halo, recognizing how
>   close is "poultry" to "poetry."
> For my fondess for near occasions of sin,
>   for all the times I wrote the names of culprits in my book
>   and sealed it shut like a shallow god,
> for all the times I take your various names
>   in vain; for all the times I pray
>   even when I am not sure
>   you are
>   not a fiction —
>   the mere fruit —
>   fragile as an egg —
>   some hope-
>   ful, woman
>   bears
>   into the world
>   full
>   of so much
>   maternal
>   material,
>   anguish
>   and so much
>   light.

Lately, I Have Been Trying To Be More

for Michael Sweeney

like the Dalai Lama
But how can I? When I feel
so Jake LaMotta.

Quinceanera

Amid Romanesque resplendence and the shadow
of Gothic lavishments, the *quinceanera* grows
impatient with the holy part.
She is dying
to file into the white stretch
limousine which idles, garish at the ready
to spirit her
and her attendants, her *damas y chambelanes*,
off to the *fiesta* her mother,
Reina de la Noche, barely having
cleared girlhood, herself, scrimped
to afford. The Queen of the Night
is young enough still to wear
the full-bodied burgundy
gown she has chosen to leave
nothing to the imagination.
It looks like something
Jane Mansfield might have been
sewn into. Her daughter,
clad nacreous like a bride, poised
on the threshold of fertility and
anguish is a virgin on the verge
of womanhood. The girl and her sharp
squad of attendants know
la misa de acción de gracias —
the mass of thanksgiving —
is a thing to be endured.
They fidget and long
for the "Go
in peace to love and serve
the Lord." for it heralds the end
of the tedium that is the sacrifice
of the mass. The *quinceanera* knows
the drill: first the sacrament,
then the party. First the sacrifice,

then the dancing; first the soul,
then the body. First the word
made flesh, then, the flesh
the word becomes. Soon
she will lay
roses at the feet of
the marble mother.
Refulgent with the glory of
ignorance, the ballsy virgin
will mouth her own "*si*,"
her gracious nod
to the unstoppable
burgeoning dawn of
fruitfulness is. Soon,
the *quinceanera* will celebrate
her own crowning,
the crowning of her waning
innocence.

          Earnest, bemused,
besotted with the exotic
bloom it is when a man gets lucky
enough to be an *extranjero* in his own
land, the Irish priest manages
his obligation to preside.
Though he seems to suppress a smirk
in the context of the involved set
of over-the-top Latina particulars,
Himself maintains
the desired solemnity; after all, he has
mastered the cleric's poker face.
He takes his best shot
at intoning the *oraciones* in pigeon *Español*,
over the girl's tiara shaped of
pearls (recalling wisdom),
and scepter (for authority),

and shoes (her long walk through life),
as the 'regulars' — Anglos, mostly —
bear curious witness from their usual spots
in the 5:00 pews. They stand
beside her in a language
they can not make out,
as the *quinceanera* bows her head
to receive God's blessing,
and the strains of God's
love for the body and
for the soul stream
into her, love
of the God who went down
and returned on the third day,
love of the voice
of the God that sings
within the body and
resounds in the temples
of the head and temple
that houses the soul,
which radiates in the larynx
and hearth of the thorax,
holding its own
light in a muscle,
brilliant and open
like a throat
engaged in song,
like a tabernacle door, open
like the body of the *quinceanera*,
fresh and made
new, open
to the strains
the soul slings,
to the body symphonic,
its meat rhapsodic,
its blossoming unbound,

its belly a hub, a bulb its soul
quickens, by which the spirit wholly
converts meat into light by the power of
love that lives within the flesh and comes
forth like cool water over rocks,
blistering as stars that nestle within
the soul, the body breathed
into, as through a kiss,
God's kiss which jump-
starts a waltz of hope
and incites a flowering
wonder sweeping
attending beholders
up in its wake.
What *extranjera* could possibly
resist such contagion?

But we Irish, we aren't really
Anglos; no, we're dark and
hopeful; the *quinceanera*
is one of us, and how
exquisite she is,
ornamented by her row
of *damas*, one more lovely
than the next, almost —
too beautiful so much so
one is tempted to look
away, put in mind, as
one is, of all the radiance
the body fails
to keep.

           And I notice
even the Irish *padre* is dashing
tonight, his complexion infused
with borrowed luster that comes

down from the apse and
pours itself upon the white
altar before refracting upwards
to illuminate his face,
as if he were the spot-lit favorite
of some cinematically inclined
angel stationed out of sight
on a granite perch and
armed with a wide angle light.
And the man too, is a kind
of angel, a good example of a guy
who's seen everything
and puts his money on the dark
horse of innocence
and the long shot
peace is.
He brings a certain obstinacy
to the table, and a modicum of
ardor to the altar where
fierce as a mick with
a grudge whose
closed fist and open
clench, like a bouquet of
fingers were made to drive
their grip into the flesh
of a lover's back;
to offer a subtle show
of power, which I
savor bearing
witness to, being
humbled by the shaky luster
of fighting the good fight, of
being all
caught up
by design,
in the molten

progression. Along for the ride
I sing and listen and feel,
and find in the moment
that nothing pleases me more
than to blow on his dice,
for I am grateful for
the proximate shillelagh
some think of as a "crutch,"
but which I see more
as a wand, or scepter
like that the *quinceanera*
carries to the altar
where she stands
before God and the Virgin
she will soon cease
to emulate as she prepares
to kneel upon her heart-
shaped pillow, and throws
down with light, thereby bitch-
slapping away the cavernous
shadow that blankets artful
hearts, hearts like shadow
Michelangelo, for instance,
tore away, like a veil or shroud,
bringing to bear all the shapely
puissance a fleshly soul provides
as it puts all it has
on light. Everything rides
on light that raves
in rock and sings
from a bush: light;
the fire of voice, light
the sculptor seduces
out of rock, light
the obstinate echo like
blood God calls from

a stone, flickering light,
invisible and blue
in daylight, light
from light, the inward
luster that seeps
out, in light
of belief without seeing, light
of seeing without eyes, true light
of true light,
the blue flickering voice,
the tongue of fire quietly
stoked, the tongue of God's
fiery mouth, God's smoldering kiss
in honor of the occasion,
in light of a world
without end
which ends
with a crescendo,
with a riot of
roses which combust
and bleed amid
clouds into sun,
amid light
that ushers in a perfect
realm wherein Desire
blooms full-blooded and pristine,
Desire, the lion, Desire, the soldier,
Desire the dove. Desire to reach beyond
the coffin's clamorous slamming shut,
Desire, a wife in the pew imagining God
made the imperfect beauty of her
flesh for love, Desire,
trying a halo on for size,
Desire the comforter,
Desire every inch
the miracle of the flesh,

Desire, penumbral and hewn of
light and meat, Desire
that turns men into Gods'
lovers with a syllable;
Desire of a city's Saturday night
princess on the brink
of childhood, taking up her scepter,
proclaiming a bold resounding
"*Si*" to all who will hear,
declaring her intention to waltz
forth into a world of fecundity and tribulation —
and her pure intention
to don a true halo of faux
pearls for the hell of it,
to step right into
sandals Jesus
would never have worn
through the streets of Jerusalem:
a pair of strappy "do-me"
sandals from Payless,
purchased for the 15th anniversary
of the girl's birth,
semi-preciously adorned
with prisms and stars
and binding strips which
confine and brandish
the intense beauty
of the *quinceanera's* painted
feet — and somehow
the shoe fits —
so the girl wears it.

Slow Air

Sometimes death comes
as a refrain. On April 28th,
my child

sang in the Music
Conservatory program
conducted in Atlantic

mall. Torment
to virtuoso t'was the
gamut. More cherub than

seraph was he, my boy,
as he let loose strains
heavenly, as if strings were being

touched — I stopped to pray
right there, on the spot, as if toward
Mecca or Medina,

outside DSW Shoe Outlet,
across from the fat lady
boutique abutting the ice

cream establishment,
ironically enough, filled
with desire but lacking a proper

spot. So I settled down
where I was.
I settled

for where I was
so my soul
could extend away

and the Divine might
venture there, enter, in-
habit the holy void

in the knowledge
that if I call
God will

come. I noticed
I was worshiping
like one who prays, ass up.

I laughed, yes,
ass up, as if upon a carpet,
five times, amid the local market place

hubbub; me, such a Mary, such a "yes
woman," such a girl
who can't say "no,"

me of so little
faith, going on fumes and pig-
headedness; emboldened

by hope, charity
unveiled — the holy
eros of "I desire

everything," fueling everything —
It's a wonder
the sacred cadences

manage past my throat and lips,
into the sailing vehicle,
the flotation device

my divine voice is able
to be, crusading crookedly,
unworthy, fast moving, slow

growing. How hard
was my prayer, that afternoon,
Holy Man, in light

of grim coincidence.
I couldn't believe
how three years, nearly

to the hour, God was doing it to you.
I know you'd say "for" not "to" —
but it was clear,

the worming
my way
inside

you had gotten inside
me; a little storm, at once
calm and boisterous,

quick and slow, was kicking
up with its odd fits and lush
starts of illumination

impossible to ignore
a tempest that vanishes
as it strikes. Instead

of candlelight
and a Gold Coast Burgundy,
Saturday night would find

Bacchus's boy choking
down the full-bodied dregs
a minute turned to vinegar.

A young heart, stopped,
a crappy *Pietà*
truth a loud procession of

warning signs
heralded was now
to yield the sorrowful

glow of a man
draped across
a woman's outstretched —

I knew that not being
surprised
even you must have felt

which was more
like being
arrested.

I knew this slow air by heart-
break and flesh. Even you
might have been

thinking, if only for a flash,
it was God
getting it all

backwards, yet I know
it is at my own peril
that I underestimate your

holiness. When it was my turn
to inform a mother she would
prepare to bury the body of her first-born son —

That wisdom I hold it
over you. You can't
grasp that, ye, of gargantuan

faith. It's the one thing
about God I can know
better than you.

When a mother —
O, we Maries —
You don't know how

we fall in love
with our boys.
When God calls

a mother
to outlive her son,
it feels like God's blunder

and no number
of angels engaged in
God's *danse macabre*

atop the head of a pin
can ease the walloping
sorrow of the crappy *Pietà*

mystery. We Maries,
we fall in love
with our sons. Abraham came

close, as if God
were aiming
to convert him into

a mother. *Adonai*
turned mother in the third
hour, and there's the sea (*Mare*),

as you know, and the Mother
we call the Church —
At your mass of

the Resurrection
I sat in Her
pews between a couple of Irish

guys, two charming
lawyers who looked
like cops or priests,

flirting venially
with each, with both,
alternating, between the two —

Who was it said "God is
in the flirtation?"
I guess it must have been me.

It's always sad at a funeral
when the guy in the vestments
steps up to the pulpit and begins:

"I did not know the deceased,"
but your dear departed didn't have
that problem. St. Camillus (patron of

the good death) smelled good that morning,
its grey-green blend of Murphy's
Oil, frankincense, hyssop and sea-worn

wood overruled by the delectable groping
stink of landed mussels wafting up off the salty
tide-whipped breeze wending its *ex-mare* way

on faint wind over the sand sailing forth
from the nebulous water like Jesus
Himself on the waves,

where men who live to live
like the moon in the waves
float and are tossed, slaves to pleasure

boats and incantation tides they adore,
who get swallowed whole
by the wild to which

they grow attached.
Funerals remind us we love
the life of the body.

When you recited "Dooney,"
I wept like the Irish poet
I am. What's in a Colleen

that makes her fall half in love
with her priest? Now don't let it go
to your head, Flanagan; I'm a Molly,

not a Brigid; I fall in love
with everyone, I'm half-mad
for love, protean as 'Jaysus'

on the waves. Maybe it's true,
guys in your line can leap-
frog all that luscious

mingling of virtue
and depravity, the sloppy
quotient that comes

with being
sculpted of meat,
but I doubt it.

I doubt
all the pee-stench
school-green hospital rooms emit

and parlors reeking of over-
ripe lilies and formalin,
and the bedside vigils —

wherein weeping kin close in —
I doubt all the Viaticum and litanies of
the saints and vicarious anguish galore

degrading flesh presents
can hammer any man who throbs
with imagination into the triumphant

neatness a starched and pristine square-inch
circumscribes, an outward sign,
like a tiny canvas worn,

like a band on the neck
of an endangered water bird,
which locks and unfastens

at the base of the throat
where song is born,
whose shell-white parameters

encapsulate and broad-
cast the glory of submission
to the notion that it all comes

forth and down
to shadow,
then peace,

that it all comes home,
that it all comes down
like love

to Kingdom come
home. I doubt that
confidence

seals a wild heart off
while setting it ablaze,
while setting a man

so neatly apart —
I doubt it works that way, Rabbi.
No, I think it's a gorgeous bout,

at best, this crap-
shoot faith, a slew of
rounds for a stubborn two-bit

punk who believes in something
to huff through —
And you — I can see you

are at your best
when you're slugging it out
like a "mick" with a temper,

quibbling with the 'work wife,'
about where the purificators belong,
or breaking down

the wall of
reverence to wisecrack
before the table ("I heard

your party was wild!")
with a spark animating
your voice and careening

through your body baroquely
clad. Or when you almost appear
to *daven* as you preside, the angel

metronome holding you
everywhere and up like
the rabbi poet you are —

it's then, you're at your holiest,
when you're rolling your eyes,
a mischievous jerk, or saying

the wrong thing —
when you're more
a disciple of Dionysus

than some green martyr —
that's where it is,
that's where

the frequency of the laughter of
that God of yours is
 palpable, visible —

And when I first came to you
that morning in the shadow
of the valley of death, all

around splayed tulips
stood erect, and burgeoning
late forsythia pushed points

sharp and blistering
yellow, insinuating their longing
substance into a new world —

As local magnolias threw themselves
open, cherry buds loosened hourly
in mighty April heat that had

come out
of nowhere, pushing out
from winter's long frigidity —

In other words, as death
clamped down,
I threw myself

at God and opened
to you; but don't
let it go

to your head, Flanagan,
reluctant Guru; God knows
I'm easy

to convert.
I didn't know
what you'd say

that April morning
when everything
in the world

had gone
wrong, but everything
you said was right.

A fine case of you,
fiddling, and God calling
the tune.

For Robo

Bodies of Water

for Scott T. Somerville

You were never a water wimp.
Even at Orchard Beach, you were good
to go. A natural swimmer, graceful
and strong. All of us were.
Natural swimmers, that is.
In water, that is.
But I was afraid to be
out over my head, afraid to swim
at dawn with you and Brutus out on 95th Street
when the lifeguard chairs were still
overturned in the sand on the shanty
"Irish Riviera" where we learned to tread water.
You always went way out.
You were never afraid
to get your ass kicked by a wave.
There was no fear
of losing control, cramping up, no fear of water
rushing to displace the spirit
of your lungs. No fear of the Earth's
humors, the protean green of its scary
unknown, no fear of the curvaceous
machine of the tides.

And how you love baths! "Tropical Rain Forest":
smoke a joint, fill the tub with aromatic
bubbles, darken the room, put music on,
pull the curtain, turn the shower on and float
away down the Nile in your vessel. You'll go
in the water anywhere. When you come out,
it's always with your head bowed down.
You shake the water off your blond head
like a dog, wearing a Miraculous
Medal, Virgin on a chain. I

never went to the beach with you
where you didn't swim.
If there was water, you went in.
At the run-down riparian patch of the Yonkers
Hudson by Ludlow Street Station,
where the hookers, junkies and "queers" congregated
you learned to fish — How I lament my sexual naiveté
(my imaginative deficit — maybe there's still time, Snow Whitey —
a few moist years — before the onset of desiccation.)
In Rockaway, we learned to swim, across
from Playland, apprentices in anarchy-cum-
juvenile delinquency on lavender boardwalk nights.
We snuck on rides, harassed arcade suckers.
It was '69, the summer my breasts arrived.
I liked that 13-year-old Tommy from Kingsbridge.
I guess maybe you did too.

In junior year at Riverdale, they made us read
The Awakening in English class. I don't remember
much about it. I read it so fast on the 20 bus.
A bored sensitive housewife takes a lover,
but it's not just a romp; it's liberty.
There was a seminal
passage about swimming and sex.
We had to dissect it
on the final. In *The Swimmer*, Burt Lancaster
searches for the true meaning of Life.
He hops over a fence and dives into
the pool that belonged to Armina,
Grandmother to Lola and Eve.
He was looking for something
he would never find. All he found
was exhaustion and emptiness
in the shallow end of the Pool of Life.
And who can forget "Daddy" in *Come Back
Little Sheba*, a chilling flick you've seen

a hundred times. Don't swim
after eating a ham. Don't dive
into a waterless pool. Don't let
a drowning victim pull you in.
Use a rope or pole.

It never mattered how cold the water was,
you'd always go in. Wappingers Falls in May,
unremarkable spots on the Sound
where I snapped that shot of you
carrying my man like a bride,
the two of you lean and fashionable
in the parking lot heat.
It was the year of the pale
pink bikini. You look terrific in your suit,
no matter how many cheeseburgers,
no matter what body
of water you swim in.
And those bedroom eyes of yours,
sleepy blue, and the curls, romantic,
emblazoned with sun like tendrils on the pate
of that lush god Bacchus, a wild spray charged
with coppery light. I first read Euripides
at age 15. At 19, I met him
in a dream. The poet was avuncular,
charming, sage, lean, more bald than grey.
Wearing a loose white robe and sandals,
he sat elevated on a great rock
overlooking the Aegean, where he entertained
a simple question I'd been puzzling over.
It concerned the huntress.
I learned Adonis does get it in the end,
a disappointing conclusion indeed:
armed huntress clobbers beauteous male love god.
Later I learned the Aegean truly is
"wine-dark," the color of dolphins, eggplants and plums,

not olive like the sand-salted Atlantic, nor Mexican turquoise,
nor your own warm favorite, your ice
blue water with its penetrable
salt, water clear enough to read through —
Jamaica — where it is your pleasure to swim and bake
beneath the dangerous sun, your nearly naked flesh
well-anointed with luxurious emollients
and fragrant French tanning products.
That day at Coney Island, I had joyous news
to break, but it was the day you became a Mermaid.
You were so wrapped up — so rapt
in the thrall of drag — your emerald
costume — your jade tail and Kelly eye-
liner, green lips and bra-straps of teal
dropping, drooping down upon your nice pair
of bare hairy shoulders, your conch shell choker
and a ratty Godiva wig.
I wanted more.
I wanted to throw you over
when the time came to sink or swim.
I wanted to jump in after you.
I wanted more of a role in your management.
I wanted to throw you
a line, but when I did, you hung up on me.
My boat capsized. It wasn't the worst
of your nefarious multifarious infractions,
transgressions, crimes, violations, no, but
there was piracy, mutiny, pandemonium on the High Seas.
Storm weathered, I shoveled out your little house on
"the Island," your little place
on the water.
I knew I was lucky
you were alive.
I knew my digging
was the sort one normally does for one's dead.
That Hollywood still, your poster of Bette and Joan,

I left it behind like a landmark,
I left it hanging like a flag on a sinking ship.
There are plenty of fish
in the sea; why shouldn't you
have all of them, Sister Girlfriend?
And I hope you know, *Stella Maris*,
I hope you know — you must know —
that come Hell or high water —
I love you madly, my wild Irish twin

Boob

1:56, 2:09, 3:43, 4:11... a digital clock flipped off
red lucent numerals in the spare charming
space where delirious with somnolence
and the accumulating lack of it,
I would enter and rock
in the blackness and
tend to those who would teach
while altering permanently
how I did it
the true value
of sleep, and its dreamy contents.
Often when I entered
watery cat-cries of appetite
and insecurity capsized
and left me weak with love-
sickness amid blue stars and
baby rabbits, in the presence of
my heart's desire
made flesh, my five-pound lovers,
their heads no larger than my heart
or fist, their fontanels not yet
having drifted to cleave like
continents sifting toward abridgment —
They needed a hand to support their necks.
They needed time to get the hang of it.
They needed official lactation expertise.
They needed me to stroke
their tongues in a flattening motion.
They needed to attain gestational age.
They needed a stubborn Irish Molly
at the helm of Operation Mammary.
They needed the bitch
attached to the hooters
to marshal her leonine defiance
when the hospital nurse and the moron

manning the La Leche phones
pissed in the new mother's milk,
saying: "A baby who takes a bottle
will never latch on." Or, as Adam
Klein extrapolating, quipped:
"Better dead, than bottle fed."
They needed me to believe
they would catch on.
They needed me to know
they would latch on.
They needed me to nurture
the hunch I'd be their lunch today,
at ages 13 and 9, had I not plucked them
from my breast at 3 like
some kinder, gentler Lady Macbeth.
They needed neither Enfamil nor Isomil.
They did not need the "Simulated Nursing System:"
consisting of tubular plastic to connect
siphoned mother's milk to nipples
designed to fool the baby —
but they needed me
to give that a shot.
What they really needed
was their mother to wear combat boots,
What they really needed was
a real motherfucker.

On those frigid January nights,
I fed a baby every hour,
every hour between midnight and that instant
when a gradual progression toward light
catalyzes rapidly and collapses
into incandescent sapphire,
so I turned to a cretin in the dark.
Though I was wholly
submissive to the issue

born of a marriage to my one
love helped along by well-stoked hope
and the alchemy of
meat and love
which bore
the *imprimatur* of a voice in the light
and my already formidable
capacity to adore
in the abstract —
I was all theirs, but
I was still mine too.
So I craved a voice
in the night with talk in it,
a cock-of-the-walk talk
that was its own voice.
I gave myself to the light
of music and love, by day, but
I turned to a broad-shouldered dope
to help me through those long nights.
He was all wrong for me,
but he was all right, too.
His was the signal through which
my maiden (*m'aidé!*)
nocturnal transmissions
had come 25 years earlier.
Electrons coming
at the speed of light,
assembling into magnetic fields
of auditory vision. I picked up
WABC in the Rockaway bungalows
through a receiver shaped like a suitcase:
my birthday gift the summer men
walked on the moon.
There were buds in the bikini top,
and an Irish boy from Undercliff
in the Bronx, out for the season.

When sand jammed the works
rendering my turntable non-
operational, Cousin Brucie came through
with the Fifth Dimension and Crystal Blue Persuasion —
In the Year 25, 25 (…if woman can survive —).

But this girl was a woman now —
And it was no longer vinyl
the station's overnight jockey was spinning
in the winter of '95 but politics.
It felt good, getting
pissed as I changed diapers,
It felt good to be disgusted
by moronic right-wing positions.
It made me feel like I still had opinions,
that a world beyond
the fruit my womb
still thrummed with
rough edges, short fuses
and a long memory:
a world well-embroidered
with prosody and music,
grit, conflict, muscle
and heat no amount of oxytocin
could neutralize. He waxed prosaic
on education, religion, government and crime;
He was a toady to the megalomaniac
Republican mayor of NY,
an apologist for the Church,
a mook in love with the "stars
and stripes," Armed Forces and "Boys in
Blue" — He was everything
I can't stand or get enough of in
a man, all rolled into a single meathead.
I turned him on, I tuned him in, I used him
each night, until my Prince came

through — until their double majesty
gained proper mastery
of their lips and tongues.
I felt ashamed,
choosing the boob over Coltrane and Mahler.
Choosing the boob over National Public Radio's
trenchant commentary. Choosing the boob
over *Sonido Suave*, Spanish lessons with a beat
you can dance to, a "*corazon*" in every strain.
Choosing the boob I saw a few times on the Uptown 5
from Utica to Woodlawn and back again.
A big dumb sexy animal with tight
T-shirt biceps and a red beret
trailed by a coterie of hot
Latino toughs: martial artists, busted-out
Crips and Bloods, leaning against the
(*Cuidado, Peligroso*. Do not lean against the
train doors.) juvie grads and unarmed hoplites
with dental gold, walkie-talkies and crude tats;
amped on bravado and justice adequate
to give a dopey half-high college girl
hurtling through the South Bronx past Mount
Eden and Tremont a false sense of
security in the middle of the night.

Becoming a mother granted no immunity
to the sexy rasp of the big dope in the dark.
There was new life, sure, but I wasn't dead.
A bad boy with a pair of pumped-up pecs
could still get to me. So I chose the boob
over Sibelius, over Dylan, over Callas.
What need had I for song?
My daylight waking hours were song
incarnate: rapturous love songs
odes to new spawn, torch songs,
aubades and serenades, arias and

songs trumpeted by haloed cygnets
bathed in dawny light — Somehow listening
to the overnight clod kept me from being
swallowed whole. I liked his trattoria spots,
how he peppered the palaver with
"*brasciole*" and "*Va Napoli!*" gleaned
from a *Barese* Canarsie pedigree. I liked the dirty
water hot dog-gobbling competition
recaps and malaprops — "credos" for "kudos" —
One night I even failed to shift to another
frequency when the overnight oaf
characterized poets and "poetresses"
as loony kazoonies and called poet Allen Ginsberg
"a perve," because I was laughing
through a certain desperation
which was a flip side of elation
in the wee hours. Footage to
counterbalance echoed in
the soft spot in my head
I reserved for idiots;
decades earlier in '79, the lug-
head had made the local *Eyewitness News*.
He was running his "deez an' doze" mouth
about Mahatma Gandhi. I enjoyed the hint
of anarchy in the mastermind behind those
mass transit "angels" who danced out the pin-
head of the chief operating boob,
who rocked the head of a pin — .
I marveled — How'd a jacked jerk like him
even know who Gandhi was?
Each night I welcomed the throwback
whose 50,000 watts of powerful sound
even the Mafia failed to silence
into my *sancto sanctorum*,
here I let him get a piece of me
in the middle of those mid-winter nights,

as I lifted one breast at a time
out of my robe, and inserted a rude
digit into baby bird mouths, bright
as gutted cherries, and squeezed
with thumb and forefinger
as if upon a trigger, aiming
to force open the jaw,
in the hope of jump-
starting the sucking reflex.
There was nothing remotely radiant or
Gerbers about this scenario —
the babies needed me to be both
muscle and nectar.
They needed me to be three parts
thug and one part Madonna.

After six weeks they latched on.
Tiny Falstaffs, they quaffed and slugged
and slurped like happy baby hogs,
nursing incessantly and in tandem.
Sometimes the twins held hands
as they drank and dozed,
capitalizing on the bottomless
amplitude of supply and demand,
bellying up to the Milk Bar
whenever the desire struck.
We didn't care who saw
or what anyone had to say.
When the kids reached for their sustenance in a cup
it was the rayon, nylon and spandex cup
of a black 34D underwire demi called "Emma."
Guys rubbernecking thought it was hot, or a threat, or both.
Once, upon watching the son glug away with gusto,
old Mary Madigan was put in mind
of a 4 year-old-she knew in County Mayo
whose family would stop by Ruddy's on Sunday after mass.

Throughout the afternoon, one would catch the boy
running about the pub looking for his mother.
Finding her, the lad would call out: "Hey Ma,
how about a suck?"

When my third child came, she knew exactly what to do;
she wasn't fifteen minutes in the material world
before she was guzzling like a field hand.
She was beautiful! I called her "Breastina."
She lived on my hip and claimed my body for her own.
I was so in love with her
I hardly fought it
when she assumed herself to be the rightful owner
of the sweater meat.
She became my "Crazy Dangerous Boyfriend."
Precocious in all things, she talked early.
When, on rare occasion, I said "no"
to the bodice ripping sprite
as she reached like a pie-eyed pirate
for my *décolletage*,
she'd engage me in dialectic,
and advocate with great eloquence
in favor of her right to nurse at will.
So much trouble to go to —
when that deep brown stare
alone would have easily done the trick.
Why argue when you can just melt
your opponent?

Le Ballon

after the painting by Puvis de Chavannes

Where are you going, maraschino star on the rise as you waft
into amber pre-dusk russet as dark looms, chasing you
down, stepping up its pace? Maybe you're the luminous defect,
O scarlet orb, the mythic rangifer's proboscis that doubles
as his navigational implement, in which case I crave your naïve magic.
Or my speed-bag heart, my cherry aloft, the sacred heart of Our Lord
(its core a hearth), the tight early bud of a young rose on a new
shoot, my last ripe egg, my clit; the diminishing returns of my fading
succulence ascending expeditious into the thermosphere, the whole
pulsating ball of wax like the insufficient adhesive Icarus relied upon,
thinking he could fly like a god without the benefit of particle collision
or an envelope billowed with warmed bluster. Or
maybe you're our own "red giant" adrift, with polar plumes and
solar flares. And why am I clad in black? How can it be that I am bound
in dark drab cloth, knickers, petticoat and hood,
lugubrious with entirely too much underwear when the bloom
of the mountains raves red and the amber sky is red and our star burns
red and I am spread open to the Heavens wishing to be borne
by hot air? Where are you headed, as you ascend like some scarlet
indication of elevated temperature through a tube drawn up into
the *caelum firmum* like diurnal *Heterocera* hunting for light banging
stupidly into what incinerates? Where, O, summer plum having
flown out from my hand like a cardinal transmitting sweetness
on waves of sound and light needing neither control blasts nor
regulators? Possibly you are a tangerine moon sharp and bold over
water observed, like film unfurling, through frames, hypotenuse
sectors, cables and girders of the Manhattan Bridge delineate,
sailing forth in search of a Navy backdrop, ascending in imperceptible
increments. Where, O commonly remarkable solar finale, raving
blossom of glory bleeding out in pathogenic metropolitan splendor,
are you going as you generously emit your deceptive glow of
methane luster hovering gorgeously over the Hudson? And who
travels forth in your vessel? Perhaps the irksome cabal of all

who have ever maligned me are assembled therein
gaining altitude as they make their way into
the ionosphere which might explain my hand on this rifle.
One well-placed shot to the globe …
Or perhaps it's a basket of boys, objects of my fascination
those I can never take or have or think of taking or having
mingled with the ones who got away,
including the several I chased off with this mighty
shillelagh and a plethora of blarney: a motley pantheon
of curious jokers, losers, beauties and geniuses:
the quotidian team: the copy shop guy, the neurologist,
the teachers, the rabbis, the poets, the ornithologist,
the News Dissector, the Big Easy painter, the Spaniard,
the morose composer, the Peruvian Soccer coach,
the blue-eyed Greek, Vaj the Geek, Ravi the bodega dude
Stein the Medievalist, the good looking Fresh
Direct guy and firefighters who wink at me on Union Street
as if I weren't old enough to be their mothers,
not to mention the schoolyard progenitors I ogle
discreetly, under the radar; perhaps they too float off
in the billowed sky-borne craft as I, pawn of depth
information and optic flow, watch the voluptuous
vehicle shrink, such that its diameter becomes
no greater than the longest segment my outstretched left hand
delineates as in my right I hold this farm implement,
broom, or spade — who knows which — as I wave farewell,
as, clutching my staff, my walking stick, sword, wand,
my rifle, I feel a fire rise — Maybe my husband is aboard
the rotund ascending object, clutching a bottle of Irish
and a couple of swimsuit models, searching
for a better wife. That wouldn't be hard to find;
she'd keep the house tidy and fuss less over the spawn;
she'd cook a meal without trashing the kitchen —
Better that, than some pain-in-the-ass Calliope running amok.
Or maybe the kids are suspended therein, *en route* to
a better mother, in which case I obviously would

refrain from cocking this baby, I would contain my fire
in the hole, and abstain entirely from taking the dirigible down,
but under such conditions my firearm would be my only friend
and the enormous sadness as they rose beyond
the exosphere and limits of "apparent" and "absolute" magnitude
headed for realms where dwell Rogue Stars, Sundogs and
Spectral Freaks, would be more blistering than any sun,
would leave me entirely deflated with nothing left
to shake my stick at. Where I would go then hardly
matters; all I know is that I would walk
softly into that auburn haze, my eyes swollen red, my heart
like a meteor, which, plummeting earthward, crashes into
the mesosphere where it self-immolates on impact,
in the end a great ball of fire
that devours itself whole.

Confessor (You Too)

I confess a dark night
is burning inside me.

Easter came,
but I failed

to open. "If I am
still so sad

in two weeks time,
I'll go for mood elevators."

I heard on the radio,
mood elevators

are in the water.
We're all on them;

what a relief!
Even you, my confessor,

assuming you take
water from the tap,

are on mood elevators.
I suppose some think of God

as a kind of mood
elevator.

As you know, the word "baptize"
means "drunk."

When first love
was lost

to me through death,
I felt my beloved belonged

to the dead.
Maybe God is not

finished persuading me.
It might shock you

to know I have written
nothing about her. I seem

afraid to look
at what I took

down
at the side of her

bed. I tell you, however,
it was as if her weight

swam off
in my mind

when you, your hand, on her
head, began: "Bernadette,

I absolve —"
In the box,

what I said, holds
true; sometimes,

being an Irish poet
is not helpful.

Senses too keen.
A charge passed through

my body, like a messenger
through the eye

of a needle — as if she were
being led out of the desert

on a camel
through the eye of

an angel, her flesh
of whose flesh

I am.
This,

versus fading,
versus ending.

I tell you,
it was

as if
her very gravity

slid off
in the mind

which is
love. I was

able to feel it
register

in my body
as light

coursing. Was
the Holy Spirit,

magnetic and tenable,
winding through me

or was I coming
down

with something?
Aloft,

on "autopilot"
all too often

when it comes to
faith, half daft,

some would
believe,

to permit
myself the rosy

luxury of loving
a loving

god, I am —
In truth,

I fall
short on faith;

I just go
on faith fumes.

I am lousy at detachment.
I envy that, in you,

the detachment.
Maybe that is

why I have not
been called to

ordination. Maybe
that is why I write

this to you, as if
writing is a kind of being called.

So you can
read it and put it

in its proper place. Who
the hell

else, might I tell,
for Christ's sake,

but detachable you,
my Irish priest? Confessor to

confessor. You know, Padre,
the song *With or Without You*

was playing on the boom-
box the moment

she died,
the Benedictine Monks'

cover of a song
by U2.

Fighting Irish

for Bernadette

In light of ordinary miracles,
renaissance, un-
easy peace,
hereby Herself
resolves:
to ride her
Beast, Venus
forth, her favor clutched
in its tombstone
teeth;
to bear
not arms but
fruit
well-spoiled;
Herself,
instrument
well touched
(of peace)
source,
Herself
of virtues, voice
of thrones, fire
grace;
neither quenched nor doused
imaginative and wise:
who opened
the womb:
firstborn,
a son,
he
of the holy
countenance

imbued with music:
Jack
perfect
in every way
that matters,
in his own world
but more
in God's
here and
now
and before and when
miracle of the body
syllable of the soul,
chord
heaven
plucks
a twin
of first love
born
Maria,
heavenly
body of the sea
ballsy Jewess
mouthing "yes"-
Miriam, "beloved one"
myrrh of sea
Maria
radiantly open
in blue light,
so serene and fierce
called after guru
Maire whose mantra —
I will —
I will be —
Thy will was
Grace,

daughter of Mayo,
warrior princess
surprise, desire,
wild Irish —
eternal baby of her
Ma — Grace,
of "the troubles"
Grace, of the Rising
ontological Grace
with cream on top.
Herself
resolves to cleave, release
and barrel forth
toward a peace of
luxury, and passion,
original
as
sin
is not —

Herself,
and her trinity, her first
love, their father —
Father, I
confess I do not know
but I know
to desire
to serve
is its own
evidence
is to crave
the unbroken
grasp that encircles
extremities
green action,
holy pulse,

nectar and percussion
muscular, silken
aglow is prize
enough
which flouts
the green drive
against
banishment —
snakes chased
into water.

Herself refuses
to live
as a slave
to Thy will
be done
unless it's
Banshee 'Jaysus'
calling the tune
upon the waves
unfathomable
yet known,
where grace is stashed
in whitecaps,
potential and kinetic in the barrels
of the waves
whose salting sinews sing
in tongues untranslatable
ferocious and kind.
O voice
of the God who turned
tables
in
the temple
ire
{Eire}

in the temple
where tender
bred
and made itself
over,
be mine!
O Banshee Jesus,
Rabbi who dances
like a wave,
his palm
full of roses and whitecaps
who throws down
the gauntlet
and opens
the door
he stands before,
who disturbs
the peace
by means
of binding
that adheres
intoxicant
round
all mothers of
light
who aspire.
O Mother,
now launched
into wind, whose laurel
fashioned of clover and intelligence,
blarney and dark light
Herself wears like a crooked
crown, a rhythmic twine
which throbs with alpha and omega,
an umbilicus through which is conveyed
the mysterious brilliance

the mixed marriage of
the human God of light to fairies
born of the bog
transmits —

Bernadette,
called after
a child who clung to her
visions;
without
knowing,
you knew how.
Without seeing
you saw,
O Warrior
Queen
of Love!
How your
mothering
survives,
your disciple
how she runs
at the mouth
like The Word
on the waves!
O charm and vessel
O navigating
tool, O grail
of one's own
design,
O parlance of
imagination's glow,
O heart, emerald
about the gills,
growing wild upon graves —
Sing in me,

earth,
suck up
the perfect
pitch
my blackness is, O
capacious Catholic realm —
Buddha, Shiva, Whitman!
O Catholic heart capacious,
your arching song
and prism of the light!

O Ruddy, towering
Colleens of savage
light
powered
by
power,
I invoke your
rough
beauty
punctuated
by spectral
measure.
 O consubstantiate voice!
O, Yeats
nut-job under the moon,
O decaying visage
still throwing off
Light!

Yes,
fire
splintering against
the night —

In light of these several
ordinary miracles,
and renaissance
which unfolds within the un-
easy peace
at hand,

Herself
hereby
resolves:
We will no longer eat
our young
whole. We
will not
die
for the Hunger
nor for any bloody Queen
in a mitre.

Up the rebels!
Transubstantiate
voice be mine!
Let our children sing!
Herself,
ordained, I —
shall take up this veil
as strangling twine
before ever I don
the bloody thing!

No blockhead (I) Herself
shall serve
as pawn
of any orthodoxy.

Herself shall show
her young
another
true
light
worthy:
belief
pure
and sculpted
of muscle
and light.

O three-quarter moon,
O ear, O quill,
unleash
 flesh, let
love —

Let love flesh
out. My eyes are smiling
but not in the way
you think.
I will grow old nodding off in a chair
beauty of my body —

Hours' fodder
who art
in Heaven
thy queendom come —

Lovers will
remember
this sacred heart
peeled away,
wherein its musical
fire is housed

its gorgeous roar
undiminished when
the beauty drains
 to be supplanted
by the beauty
that follows
as the sediment sinks and
the Omega rises — O
Muse
at the checkpoint,
loaded for meter,
gilded with light,
shillelagh at the
ready.

Ready to dance
curvaceous,
ruddy at the hearth
before which
your daughter
Herself is,
an Irish poet
tingling with restlessness
blessed with heat,
armed with resiliency,
warming up,
her pipes.

God
in her
corner
with Her
Irish up
and Herself,
in God's.

Note well and heed
our own Bernadette Agnes,
at stage left; bitching
 about the bishop, and the war
her cretin king is hosting.
She does a mean
"Stack of Barley."
She's along for the long
haul and sheer
joy-
   ride —

Jesus
wanted
dead or alive,
whose soft
bird of fire —
whose
tongue
in her
ear,
urges:
go out
to sing
the world.
His heart is a fist
of lyric
in bloom.

Herself (I)
refuse to be
dragged down
to drown
in the bog
that is the easy

analysis.
 God's lover,
Herself
I have found
favor
with

what
I love

will

hold

me

like a wave on the sea.

O pipe, O whistle,
O bagpipe, O bag
of waters!

Up the rebels, Brigids,

Let's see you dance
out of the bag,
and run at
the mouth,
and intone
and declaim
and snarl
at the regular changeable pearl
the moon is
an opening
in the blackness,
in open air.

Fiddle as Rome
is reborn!

Mollies unbound,
turned out;
which side
are you on?
Powered
as you are
by the green
tenacity of lust and
white heat of
love.
Slainte! Here's to

God's hard
and gorgeous

world —

Get up.
Good night Gracie.
    Slainte
        Slainte
            Slainte,

I'm not going
anywhere; I'm just going
everywhere
so as to cast
this blue-green
gaze
like a line,
this fine line

like
grace —
on life —
　on death —

　　　　Get on with it.
　　　　　　Get it up.
　　　　　　　　Giddyap.
Horsewoman,
Piss off!

Capularis *

To put one's affairs in order,
to ponder and articulate,
to ejaculate and swim,
to lug, muddling,
the heavy bodies
our minds are
through emulsifying
tedium and industry,
to be all ears,
to have eyes
in the back of our heads,
to wear our hearts on our sleeves,
to be operatic and porous,
submissive to susceptibility,
mounted by curiosity,
to invite wonder,
to wander 'round
castles of our own
making, modest, yet baroque,
to capitalize upon the acoustic plenty
we find therein, to ambush our muses,
to push them up against the wall,
as, sultry, domineering and
obedient to octave shifts and
crescendo we commit
to memory and come
to know song by heart,
to consent to being governed by vision,
by seeing what sticks
to the wall when we
catapult it, to fling
our souls into the ring
like a line into surf,
like the flesh of a tomato
going up against

ancient granite,
is to sing ourselves to dream.
And when we sling our souls
forth, their ripe mettle combusts.
Chains sound, the drawbridge
is lifted and towering carillons
resound as accompaniment
to our crossing over into the life of
hurtling death we live
which finds its way into
the concerto. It's our occupational hazard
to guess. But in any case
the scherzo's on us.
There's no getting around it.
You're always Keats or Yeats,
young in middle-age, immature
in dotage, dashing, in your way,
on your own, in your own way,
your own worst enemy,
your own insurance policy.
Sure, you were fluid once,
but in the end, you are fluent.
If you are lucky, you are
venerable but lust
still, not dead
on the beach,
a good looking corpse,
your work in crates,
your joy disseminated,
attaching where you never would
have expected, the incantations
of your divine tribe taking root
underground, in bloom,
a sharp-looking legend,
whose work is perfectly laid

down upon cross-
thatched cross-
hairs — all fruition, friction,
and operatic luster
(*"Da mi colori!"*)
who were once wily and outsmarting,
with a fine command of perspective,
an all-knowing god in tight pants,
peeling off, flexing jacked-up imagination,
guns out. If you are still here,
still listening, maybe you're venturing
to guess that maybe lumbering
the distance, unencumbered
by all the times you didn't get it
right, or get it down
is possible. Growing old,
once an anathema,
is looking pretty
good about now.
The rope-a-dope
tuckers one out,
naturally, but you're still
fighting Irish
when the bell goes off,
you go off into action,
pummeled as you are
into an ample tenderness.
You're a great white dope
in love with the holy
Word. In the
mix, you are
in the
clear as a bell's
echo, delicious
in your way,
no longer in your own way,

armed with ornery
fervor and a few
worthy combinations capable
of ripping away whatever
ropes you're up against.
You make a loop of their twine
to fashion not a noose
but a curved means of reining in
stars to gather as you gallop
toward the celestial vault
that you might
do with them
what you will —
You're a god,
peeling
away, like a bell,
pealing, off,
you're a little
off, in your chariot, leaving
not enough blood
to kill you behind
where it mottles
the canvas, its contours indicate
the shape of crescent
moon burnt in orange,
the color of oxidation,
the ruddy color
of your Irish up,
a revisionist moon
up and ripe
for raving at,
a red moon
to remind you
that maybe waning is waxing,
automatic or waxing lyrical —
maybe it is just

as well beauty
is sacrificed
like a firstborn child
on the altar of faith
by willing participants,
the dumb chumps
who go along
with a cruel joke
a stuttering god articulates
as lust yields but is wasted
on the young,
and suckers like us
with all our expertise
in beauty who stand
by, gaping and open,
say precious little
more than "Wow!"
with our Irish up
gaining greatest altitude
just
as the glow begins
to vanish from our flesh,
and the elasticity, which
resiliency can replace,
moves out of our
reach — but maybe
waxing is waning,
maybe beauty is nothing
more than a series of tests and
lavishments a hot and
cold running muse delivers
in a whorl without end —
a world with no end
in sight, a ravishing world
overgrown and lush,
through which,

advancing, we prance,
as, besotted with a certain fidelity
to these savory cuts of music
and the study of pulchritude
on the run, as, besotted
with fixations on surprise,
shadow, wit, mindfulness and song,
as, hounded and trumped
by a fascination with what's difficult,
we keep travelling, stuck
on trains of thought so glorious
who *but* a poet could possibly
know how to catch one?
We accelerate and thrum,
figuring, who but a poet
can be trusted
to conduct crucial
interviews with the engineer?
Who can be trusted
to conduct the strange adaggio,
say, of equinocturnal snow
such as this one I behold,
which in turn takes hold
of me this instant
as it transpires outside
my window
as inside the chambers
of this poet's heart
which is one busy
pump tonight?
The flakes fail
to sail straight
but rather they slalom
curvaceous in a downward
waltz at the behest of
gravity, their lacey

voluptuousness aglow
as they tumble and land
with an unheard thrash
upon early shoots of hell-
bent crocuses, which may be
seen and construed
as the frozen upshot of
God's shooting from the lip,
the aftershock only poets
even if nodding off
in chairs before fires
making love in their dreams
can hear, for their fires are still
going below, their pilot
lights are still blue:
their angel vehicles are still
aloft as ever, eternal dirigibles
amid a marbled firmament, afloat
in a variegated field
of nacreous noctilucence,
amid the ramous circuitry
that reminds me a bit
of those black limbs
encased in ice
my neighborhood pear
tree brandishes; they
overlay an under
drawing which burns
with astonishing ordinary
beauty in my icy fenestral vista:
a modest scene adequately
lovely to incite lachrymal
wetness, depicted, as if in oil,
which right angles and
perimeters my window frame,
delineate, limit and set

apart. Glassed-over
rounding off of new buds
frozen in clear swells
form barely visible molds
of ready green that reached
early from shoots but stopped short,
stunned in the frigid clench
of a casement that is doomed
to cave in under
the weight of light
and the warmth
its live limbs dispatch
in the interest of releasing
dormant verdure from its trans-
lucent, transparent confinement
giving way to an arching rhapsody
of swollen tips, lips, fists
against the death winter
doesn't always have to be.
A bright backlash follows
having waited so long
for the "go ahead" —
The waxing heat
comes as it may,
comes as it can,
armed with explosive
wetness and romping
pulse with which we,
O, supple bards,
have some sense of
what to do. It is for this
reason we may decide
we might be wise
to stick around a while
if only to see
what develops,

knowing all
too well
the inspiration
that is ours
doesn't come
cheap,
but it comes.

Capularis is Latin for "having one foot in the grave."

The Other Side

Not far from Croagh Patrick and Mountain of the Eagle
where the patron saint fasted 40 days
praying for the salvation of the Irish people,
in a country you rarely called "home,"
for you attached little affection
and none of that shanty inflection
so many Greenhorns favored —"On the other side,"
in 1900, the year Oscar Wilde died, you were born;
but being no great lover of books, not even the Bible,
which the Pope forbade the faithful to read,
you wouldn't care about Wilde any more than for parsing
the gospels direct. That would have been rough going
for you, Mary, with your two years of school, yes, just
two years of school, then it was off to the lace factory,
which you called "the lace school." No, "Oscar Wilde"
would not ring a bell, though queens made you giggle;
and didn't matter to you any less or more than
history or science: them "silly things ... for important people
best t' be bothering with." The Marquess of Queensbury,
creator of the rules of pugilism imprisoned Irish fairy, Wilde,
across the sea, as in "the States" the Labor Party was coalescing
powerfully, Tammany Hall was the Irish king of your
New York circa that 1900th year of Our Lord,
and you were born. Once you crossed and became
American, a quarter of a decade later, you eschewed political
concerns. A suffragette's nightmare, you were —
First Tuesday, each November, Mike would rattle
the marital bed, rousing you early, "Himself" propelled by civic
fervor such as only the freshly naturalized possess, he'd lead you
off to the Public School to wait in line to vote Democrat as did he,
to which obedience widowhood at 50 put an end. At the parish
Golden Age Club, later on, local 'pols' vied for your vote.
I too, tried electioneering in a hope to sway you, but
politics held as much interest for you as physics or greed.

Hell, born dirt poor 50 years after "The Hunger," you hadn't a thing
against Brits. And so hard were you, Mary,
of hearing, that by the time the Roman Church
had done away with the Latin, you couldn't even hear it
when the priests told the faithful how to vote
from the pulpit. You missed the whole
bloody homily for years! Had you heard, you would have heeded
Father, for any priest was better than no priest, and
a crooked one was as good as any
for a "special intention"; so long
as you put your envelope in the Sunday basket on a stick.
Any priest, even a queer priest or a drunken one, could well put in
a good word with Our Lord. Friedrich Nietzsche
died on the continent the week you were born near Lough Mask and
Knock, where the Blessed Virgin magically appeared, not far
from *Cong*, and *Fir Bolg* where a race of small dark pagans
mated with the fairer tribe *Tuatha de Denaan*, in a wood
frequented by fairies. Wilde? Nietzsche? Neither would
interest you, for philosophers were good
for about as much as poets, or atheists or queers.
And though you were crazy about God, your strong
overriding preference was for his mother.
You never learned to speak to either of them direct,
but mastered the speed-rosary decades faster than the godspeed
of light! But unlike so many American Irish, you
never let the Holy Roman Church succeed in making you
mean. In the 1900th year of Our Lord, prospectors were flocking
to the Klondike, and laborers were breaking
ground on the streets of New York where Paddy "sandhogs'
dug out those subway tunnels wherein your mate would spend
a third of his life in the dark as a man with a steady job.
He was born in the city, a lad from Limerick, but you,
you were born where the Armada first touched land;
where Christ's Spaniards and pirates armed with ferocious

darkness paused to plunder and sully the chill,
pallid grey-eyed Colleens, leaving their white
seed and indelible pitch behind, like tattoos borne in blood —
A blackness which descended down to me,
for which I thank you.

About the Author

Michele Madigan Somerville is the author of the book-length poem *WISEGAL* (Ten Pell Books 2001). Her verse has appeared in *Hanging Loose, Mudfish, Pagan Place, Downtown Brooklyn* and *Puerto Del Sol*.

She won first place in the W.B. Yeats Society poetry competition in 2000 and a MacArthur scholarship for poetry at Brooklyn College in 1987. A native New Yorker, she taught for many years in New York City elementary and high schools, in the City University of New York, and at the State University of New York, Purchase College. She lives in Brooklyn with her husband and three children.